I0436919

Stop The Bus!

A straightforward, down-to-earth guide to help you assess your life so that you can make the most of your "journey" ahead.

by

Anne Harper

Bloomington, IN   Milton Keynes, UK

authorHOUSE®

AuthorHouse™
1663 Liberty Drive, Suite 200
Bloomington, IN 47403
www.authorhouse.com
Phone: 1-800-839-8640

AuthorHouse™ UK Ltd.
500 Avebury Boulevard
Central Milton Keynes, MK9 2BE
www.authorhouse.co.uk
Phone: 08001974150

© 2007 Anne Harper. All rights reserved.

*No part of this book may be reproduced, stored in
a retrieval system, or transmitted by any means
without the written permission of the author.*

First published by AuthorHouse 3/20/2007

ISBN: 978-1-4259-8676-6 (sc)

Printed in the United States of America
Bloomington, Indiana

This book is printed on acid-free paper.

Dedication

I dedicate this guide to Mrs Mitchell who inspired me to write it. "Life is an attitude of mind, focusing on the good and the road ahead" she once said to me. At 94 years old she shouted a week after arriving at her Nursing Home "get me out of here - it's full of old people". Guess who was the oldest?

Contents

1. Stop the Bus

At the ripe young age of 39 I was going through what was ultimately called my 'mid life crisis', acting and feeling as if I was twenty while underneath scared of hitting the big four 0.

Since graduating from University my life had centred around my career as a hotel manager and bringing up my two children, who were by then eleven and thirteen and already showing signs of independence. As my birthday loomed ever nearer I was definitely aware that another chapter of my life was about to start.

But what will it be? Where was I going? What would it be like?

I saw my life as a road in front of me, half of it anyway, the other half is behind. Scared of not making the most of the road ahead and losing what is most precious to all of us – **TIME.** I decided to take a closer look at my life and asked myself some questions:

- Who am I?
- Where am I going?
- What am I going to do?
- Who was I going with?
- How was I getting there?
- What problems might I encounter on the way?
- More importantly, how can I enjoy the journey?

This uncomplicated, easy to understand book has been designed to help you analyse your life, so that you can make the most of your road ahead, just as I did.

2. The Travelled Road

Imagine yourself standing on your road of life looking behind at the route you have already travelled. I assume that you, like me, have already clocked up many miles behind you. Many of these miles may have been smooth however, since life is not always perfect, your road may have had many pot holes and rocky patches.

As you stand on your road, do you dwell on what is behind you, mind in the past but body in the present, thinking of previous failures, focusing on the mistakes you have made? Or do you re-live happy memories that you wish had not passed and cannot re-kindle? When my road hit a rocky patch I used to bury my head in the sand or find something to distract my mind rather than facing up to what has gone wrong or what I could do to fix it – do you do the same?

To be able to live in the present with confidence and contentment you need to make peace with the past. What I have done is to look closely at the road behind me and start to face up to:

- What I am holding on to.
- The mistakes that I have made.
- The happy times that I kept recalling and would not let go.
- The resentment that still boiled inside me.

By understanding the past I was then able to learn from my mistakes, accept that I cannot change or alter the past and finally... **move forward into the future.**

What have been the rocky patches – highs and lows of your life so far?

Examples could be:

Highs	Lows
• Passing exams • Learning to drive • Family days out • Holidays • Buying a car • Promotion • Getting married • Starting a family • Special days with friends • Achieving your best at your chosen sport golf/ swimming/football	• A family death • Relationship ending • Bullying • Illness • Relationship choices • Debt • Misuse of alcohol or drugs by you or others • Losing your job • Unhappy childhood

Complete your highs and lows (see over)

Highs	Lows

After I completed my table of highs and lows I realised that there were far more highs in my life than there had been lows. Yet here I was focusing most of my time and energy mulling over what had gone, reliving them again and again, blaming myself, for things that had gone wrong.

I learned from looking at my list that it was the choices I made that caused most of the lows. These choices I now see had been largely due to my low self esteem, choice of partners or remaining in jobs for far too long because I was scared to move on.

There had been some very low points in my life -emotional bullying that I had received at school ,and the debilitating post natal depression after my first child was born. It was only as I tried to understand why these lows affected me so badly, that I was able to see that I had no control of these individuals behaviour nor my hormones. Yet in the past I had convinced myself that I was the cause and I was to blame.

My high-lights of my life ranged from moments of joy from the birth of my children, picnics with my family to achieving my qualifications and starting my own business.

As I noted all my high points what surprised me was the fact that I accepted all these brilliant events and days but never really **appreciated** them at the time – probably still focusing on the bad times.

Not any more as now I live in the present. I have a list of all my achievements, happy memories, my strengths and the compliments that I receive in my diary. While I certainly **do not dwell on the past,** on the 'not so good days' I can look up these reminders. It is amazing the effect that just looking at this list has on me: I feel more energised, confident and an immediate sense of achievement. This gives me the strength to cope with those 'not so good days'.

The lows – well they're in the bin where they belong – **in the past!**

- What do you keep "holding on to"/looking back at?

- Why?

- What have you learned from looking back?

- What will you do differently now?

- What did you learn from assessing the lows?

- What if anything, can you do differently in the future?

- What was it about the highs that made them "high"?

- What did you do to achieve these highs?

- How did you feel?

- What, if possible, can you do to make you feel this way again in the future?

3. Who am I?

We are all very **unique** with different attitudes, strengths, beliefs and values. The people we knew in the past, and the genes we have inherited from our ancestors, have influenced us and help shape us into the people we are now.

Who were the main influences in your life?

My main influencers were my parents, best friends, teachers, neighbours, college lecturers and fellow students (especially those I shared a flat with) and, more recently, my boss and husband.

Who were the main influencers in your life?

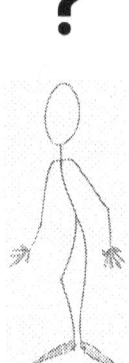

Looking back at my early years and assessing those who moulded me into the person I now am, I was amazed to realise that there were many who definitely had a <u>negative</u> impact on me.

The worst was my English teacher at secondary school. Her attitude towards me was dreadful. She ridiculed me in front of my peers particularly about my lack of intelligence. As a result I lost confidence in my abilities and in myself. In fact, it has taken many years to realise that there are many types of intelligence and that being academically brilliant is <u>not</u> the be all and end all.

Another person whose behaviour impacted on my life was my childhood best friend Jill. Jill and I were inseparable since the age of four. Her house was across the road from mine and we were in the same class at school. We used to play, walk home from school together, our families even went on holiday together. So you can imagine the shock when at the age of 16 I was suddenly 'dropped' as Jill's best friend for no apparent reason. She would not walk home with me, sit next to me or even talk to me. She only had time for Stacey – her 'new' best friend! During this time my father, whom I was very close to, died unexpectedly. The loss of the two people that I had loved, depended on, confided in and spent most of my time with had a profound effect on me for the rest of my life and had an enormous impact on my other relationships. I no longer trusted others not to leave me and also found it hard to build friendships as I was scared of losing them. I became a doormat, - never standing up for myself and often ending up in situations I should never have been in.

Several years later Jill and I met. She explained her behaviour very simply, "I knew I was a lesbian and you were not. We were different, how could I tell you?" I only wish she had, I would have understood and been there to support her.

My main role model was definitely my mother - my mum is one in a million. After my father died she was so supportive to me and my brother, never showing her grief to us. She enrolled on a college course and changed her career. She coped well with selling the house and re-locating. She even started her own business – 4 florist shops - and is still successfully running one of them at the age of 70. My mum is fiercely independent and copes with anything that life throws at her and always with a smile!

- Who were the role models in your past?

- What were their good points?

- What was their impact on your life?

- What can you do to be more like them?

- Who drained the life out of you or pulled you down?

- What were their bad points?

- How did their behaviour impact on your life?

- How can you be different from them?

4. The Bus

As you travel down your road are you alone? I have various people that I am in contact with – family, friends, work colleagues, those I share my hobbies with and people who 'drop in and out'.

Have you ever really thought about those you share your thoughts, ideas, laughs and hardships with? What is it about these individuals that make you keep in contact with them?

Why do you keep in contact with them?

What are the characteristics, qualities and behaviours you look for in others? For example, this is what I look for in others;

- Good listener
- Fun to be with
- Shoulder to cry on

- Supportive
- Enthusiastic
- Great conversation
- Hard working
- Shared interests

What qualities and behaviours in others are you attracted to?

-
-
-
-
-
-
-
-
-

5. Your Bus

Imagine that every person you share your life with is on a bus (double decker, single, bendy, open-top entirely up to you).

To do this exercise you must empty the bus and have everyone you know stand in a queue at the bus stop – family, friends, work colleagues, associates etc.

Visualise yourself standing at the door of the bus about to welcome everybody standing in the queue back on board. As you shake each person's hand ask yourself "what qualities, behaviours, and characteristics does this person have that helps me on my life's journey?" Think very carefully as you invite them on board.

There may be someone's hand you are standing shaking thinking "why are you on my bus?" "All you've done is take, while I've given. You are draining the life out of me". This could be the colleague who's always complaining that nothing is ever right or the 'friend' who borrows but never returns and certainly never says thank you.

What are you going to do now?

Invite them on or leave them at the Bus Stop!

It is your choice!

When it comes to family and relatives, the saying goes "you can choose your friends but you can't choose your relatives". It may be, as you shake someone's hand, you realise "I don't want .... on my bus". You may have to consider "what do I need to do to ensure that I can feel at ease with .... on my bus especially for the sake of the family".

When I did this exercise I realised I did not want my uncle on my bus. He was always complaining, ruined Christmas for me every year with his criticising and negative attitude. He would never show his appreciation for anything I gave or ever did for him; he just picked on me.

After completing this section I decided that I needed to address this situation. I went round to see him and asked why he treated me the way he did and told him of the affect it was having on me. He told me that I reminded him of his Grandmother who helped bring him up but who had died without him saying good-bye. As he was talking, he slowly realised that the anger and guilt that he felt he was transferring on to me.

From that day on we were able to establish a much better relationship with this new understanding and he is back on my bus.

After completing this section you may have identified some people who you decide that you do not want on your bus. By identifying the problems, speaking to them and listening to their answers you can sometimes try to understand how they are feeling and maybe start to see things from their point of view. As a result of sometimes confronting issues, it may allow you to come to a compromise and therefore make you more comfortable about having them on your bus -especially family members who you <u>have</u> to have on your bus for the sake of others.

6. Who is on Your Bus?

Take your time with this session. Draw your bus and put everyone you want on your journey in your bus and as you write their names, or draw their faces, think of the reasons why they are important to you and how they enrich your life.

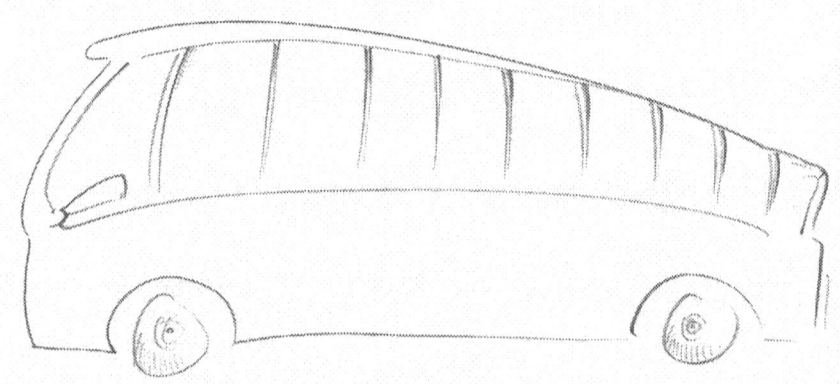

• Who have you left at the bus stop?

- Are you going to do anything about it?

- Are there empty seats on your bus?

- What type of person/s would you like to fill your seats? E.g. someone who is a good listener? Someone who enjoys a great night out? Someone who has the same interests as you do?

- Why are they not there?

- Where are you going to find them?

- Who have you lost contact with that should be on your bus?

- What are you going to do?

- Who is on the bus that enriches your life?

- Are you taking them for granted?

- How are you going to make them feel appreciated?

7. Whose Bus are You on?

Buses work both ways!

It would be great to think that everybody I have on my bus has invited me onto theirs. We all have different strengths, qualities and behaviours that attract others to us.

When I first did this exercise many years ago I can truly say I did not like me. I would not have invited myself on my own bus far less anyone else's. Short-tempered, slightly depressed, often criticising, no 'sparkle' - no wonder I was not invited on many buses.

Once I had really taken a hard look at myself I was able to see where I could improve and with the help of this book I am happy to say that I am definitely on board several other buses.

We are not all perfect – I know that I can be slightly selfish, over opinionated, bossy and dizzy at times.

By knowing where your behaviour is letting you down you can address and improve it – if you want to!

I do have more positive qualities – enthusiastic, loyal, encouraging and caring.

- What positive qualities, behaviours and characteristics do you have that others may appreciate and would encourage them to invite you on their bus?

- What are your less favourable attributes that might make others decide to leave you at the Bus Stop?

- What can you do to ensure that you are invited onto the buses that you would like to be invited on to?

8. Atmosphere on the Bus

What is the atmosphere like on your bus? Lively?
Sombre? Energised? Quiet? Or a little bit of
all this and more?   There are times in our lives
when we need a little bit of peace and quiet or
a fun night out.   It's the variety of people we
know and have in our lives that can provide this
atmosphere as well as your own personality.
Balance is the key.

What is the atmosphere when you are around?

Do you bring a breath of fresh air into a party?
Does laughter radiate from the staff room? Or
are there glum faces staring at you?

What you give is what you get - most of the
time!

When I worked in the hotel I was able to tell what the atmosphere would be like that evening just by looking at the rota.

If Sally was working we would be in for a great night. She was always pleasant, smiling, chatting to the customers and hard working.

If, on the other hand, Michael was on, the atmosphere would be sombre and tense. Everything was a problem, he continually moaned – if it was sunny he'd be too hot, if it was raining it would be too dull and wet. Every cloud had a black lining. No wonder the bar was quiet the nights he was on.

What is the atmosphere on your bus generally?

- At home

- At work

- With family

- With friends

- What do you appreciate about the atmosphere?

- Who controls it?

- If need be, what can you do to alter it?

9. Who is in the Driving Seat?

Now look at your bus. Where are you? At the back having a party? Sitting looking out of the window in a daze? Or chatting to others not knowing which route the bus is taking or where it is going? Or are you in the driving seat knowing your destination, the route your bus is taking and in control?

There may have been different people sitting in the driving seat at various times of your life, your husband, mother, daughter, boss or friend!

A colleague of mine, Pamela, came to me after reading my first draft of the booklet to tell me her story of how she had been affected by others driving her bus.

She explained that her very domineering mother had controlled her life when she was young, choosing her subjects at school and her interests, never allowing her freedom to invite her friends round. She even applied to the university that she thought her daughter should attend and picked her courses.

When Pamela started university she was 'lost' and found it extremely hard to live her own life. Making choices was not something she'd been used to. It was not long before she met Brian - 'the control freak' as she called him.

Pamela had replaced her controlling mother with Brian, who was even worse! He chose her clothes, hairstyle, food, how long she could study for, the film they would see and so on. Except with Brian came the put downs. He criticised her constantly with comments like "you can't spell", "you look terrible in that", "you didn't deserve that grade".

At 25, and after five years with Brian, Pamela said she looked and acted like she was so much older, with no mind of her own, cut off from all her friends and with no confidence at all.

Pamela finally went to the doctor after she had a breakdown. She felt worthless, a total failure with nothing to live for. The doctor explained she was suffering from depression and suggested a course of anti depressants and counselling.

Several months on, after many counselling sessions, she came off the anti depressants, ejected her driver (Brian) and firmly placed her own bottom on her driving seat. For the first time in her life she was in CONTROL.

Fifteen years on Pamela is happily married to Peter and has two children. As she says: "I'm driving my own bus, Peter is driving his bus and together we're driving the same route."

All I ask you to do at this stage is to really consider:

- Are you the driver of your bus? If not who is driving your bus?

- Why have you allowed this person to sit in the drivers' seat?

- Who makes the most important decisions about your life?

- How do you feel when you are not in control?

- Why is it important to be in the drivers' seat?

Now consider what changes you may have to make to ensure that you are in the driving seat and in control of your own life. You don't have to make big changes immediately to make an impact, but small alterations can make a difference straight away.

For example, saying "No" – being positive sometimes means having to say no.

"Sorry I cannot make it for tea this Sunday mum".

"Thank you for asking me onto the committee again this year but unfortunately I will have to decline".

"I do sometimes enjoy watching sport on the television but this evening I will be watching a drama on the other side".

By saying no you are already beginning to make a difference to your life.

Taking control of your life is ensuring that <u>you</u> are the one making the decisions, not someone making them for you, and being happy with the choices you have made. Life is full of compromises - giving and taking - and being considerate of others may mean that you are doing something that you personally may not want to do. However <u>you</u> should be the one that says yes or no, not someone else.

Sometimes you can rely on a person/people too much, perhaps to make decisions for you or map out your road ahead as <u>they</u> see it. They may not always be there, or make the right choices for you, but at least <u>try</u> taking control, **sometimes**.

10. Out of Control!

There may be times when you <u>feel,</u> or possibly <u>are</u> out of control.

Your behaviour becomes excessive – this can be anything from drink and drug abuse, late nights, affairs, and acting out of character.

A close friend of my brother's, John went 'out of control' after his wife left him for another (younger) man.

People can react very differently to this type of situation – perhaps hiding away and becoming depressed, but in this case John went out socialising, drinking and gambling whenever possible.

Not wanting to spend his nights in at home alone John went out drinking every night, usually to the local bar. As time went on his drinking became heavier, and after being at the local pub he would venture into the city and end up at the casino - drinking more and spending money he definitely did not have.

"During this period of my life I was "out of control" he said.

"Was I driving my bus? – Oh no. I was at the back of the bus thinking I was having a whale of a time – socialising, drinking and gambling - but not really knowing why! That is until my bus nearly crashed! I was heavily into debt, most of my 'friends' had stopped speaking to me and worst of all I had been so drunk one night I collapsed and had to be taken to hospital with a broken nose, cuts and bruises. I had no idea how it had happened – what a wake up call! I just couldn't see how depressed, lonely and out of control I had become".

With the help of his sister, John sat down and re-assessed his life. They contacted the Citizens Advice Bureau who were able to give him vital advice on managing his money and consolidating his payments.

He contacted the local rehabilitation centre and got therapy and help so he could to 'dry out'.

Since then he has attended Alcohol Anonymous for over two years and to this day is still alcohol free.

He moved back into his driver's seat and headed more sensibly down the road of life, with a few apologies to those he had neglected, ignored and hurt in the process.

It was the realisation that he was no longer in the driving seat that made John take stock of his life. Nobody was!   He was 'out of control! His bus had been veering in the wrong direction and heading for a head on collision. That caused him to put on the brakes, sit in the seat and take control. John has now joined several clubs – hill walking and golf - and has even run the local 10K for charity. He has still to meet someone special but he is now enjoying his life filled with new, and old, friends (and plenty of fresh orange juice!).

• Have you ever been out of control?

- Why did this happen?

- Were you aware that you were out of control?

- What are you going to do to ensure that it does not happen again?

- What lessons did/have you learned?

11. Baggage

Now that you have filled your bus with the people that you need on your journey through life, what about the baggage!

As you look on the roof of your bus is it weighed down with all the baggage, i.e. worries and troubles: the mortgage, debt, an ill relative, the child that is abusing drugs, work that never seems to end – the list can be endless!

There are times when I'm sure you can hardly manage to move your bus due to the weight of your baggage.

I have a very close friend whose bus was, and to some extent still is laden down with baggage.

Over six years ago my friend finally left her disastrous marriage with her two children, then aged 4 and 6. Her husband had had several affairs during their marriage and often gambled. It was not until after she left him, that she became aware of the severe debt he had accumulated - he had re-mortgaged the house in her name to finance his gambling addiction.

With very little money, debtors knocking at her door and with no job and two small children she had to sort out her baggage.

Her bank manager was very helpful, assisting her to take control of her financial situation. He set up direct debits for all out going payments so that she knew how much she would need to make each month. Her parents and friends helped look after her children so that she could go back to work. I sat down with her and worked out what her strengths were and we were able to identify how, and where, she could get a job that would earn her enough money. After many letters and three interviews, she was offered a secure job.

She filed for divorce and soon met a very special person who is still in her life today.

Her road has not been smooth and the baggage still weighs her down. For over four years she received no money from her ex husband. He chooses to hardly ever seen his children, not turning up to take them out on the days he was supposed to have them, forgetting their birthdays, cancelling holidays, leaving her to pick up the pieces.

I admire her for her strength, her ability to cope with any given situation, to never speak ill of her ex in front of her children and, most importantly, for never giving up.

- What does your baggage contain?

- Take a closer look at the contents of your baggage rack. Is there any way that you can lighten the load?

Baggage.

- Who can you contact?

- What help is available?

- Who can you share your problems with?

12. Fuel Tank

A real bus needs fuel to make it move. Without it it would stop, go nowhere, grind to a halt.

It goes without saying that you too require fuel to run efficiently and cope with the extra baggage.

This type of fuel is the kind that ensures that we have the strength to keep going, the attitude to keep focused.

What gives you energy?   What makes you feel good, gives you confidence and oomph!

- I fill my tank by:
- A walk in the country
- A long bubble bath
- Playing football with my son
- Dancing
- A game of golf with friends

- A great night out
- Having a laugh
- Going to the Gym
- Shopping with my daughter

Keep your tank full!

Most of what I do to keep my tank full you may consider being selfish – it is not, it is being SELFLESS. Without it I know my tank would be empty and my bus would grind to a halt.

Several years ago I was diagnosed with depression. I had given up work as a hotel manager to be a full time wife and mother. I spent the first year after leaving work feeling very isolated and under valued.

Feeling extremely low I finally went to see my doctor. I sat and poured my heart out to him. He patiently listened to me before he wrote out on his prescription pad.

"GO BACK TO WORK!"

He then said "You gain your energy and strength from people – go fill up your tank!"

I then found a part-time job that involved training others within the hospitality industry. The job also helped me take control of my finances, boosted my self-esteem and gave me back a feeling of worth.

I also enrolled in badminton classes once a week and joined two mother-and-toddler groups. Many people, including my mother, kept saying I was being selfish. Not at all! I was now pouring energy into my once dry tank and discovered that not only was I now being able to cope with my baggage but valued my time with the family more.

What gives you energy? – Fill your tank!
-
-
-
-
-

13. Roundabouts

Everyday, every hour, in fact nearly every minute of the day we come across a roundabout in our lives. These are decisions that have to be made. Some are very easy – what am I having for tea? What TV programme will I watch tonight? Some are extremely difficult - will I change my job, end a bad relationship or when will I retire?

In life you will often see a roundabout ahead, while some circumstances are thrust unexpectantly upon you e.g. redundancy, illness or even promotion.

As you progress towards the roundabout this is what I call thinking or analysing time. Sometimes you can go round and round and round the roundabout, analysing and reanalysing, to the point of 'paralysis by analise. Decisions can be very hard to make, especially ones that can affect not only your own life but the life of those very close to you. I have frequently heard friends saying:

"What would happen to my children?"

"How will I cope with juggling work and family?"

"What will be said about me?"

"How can I cope with the extra pressure?"

"What will I do with all this extra time?"

- Are you stuck on a roundabout?

- What decisions have you to make?

In these situations I believe in writing a list of advantages and disadvantages. That way it can be easier to come to a conclusion. Asking others for advice or listening to their opinions can also be helpful. But remember, it will ultimately be your decision, not theirs.

Make a list of all the advantages/ disadvantages which may help you come off the roundabout.
(see next page)

Advantages	Disadvantages

Roundabouts can occur when we have a life changing road to choose. They can appear at certain times in our lives - at birthdays, changing job, children leaving home, retirement etc.

It is at times like these that you may be forced to reassess your life and choose which road to take

"Where am I going?"

"Where do I want to be?"

"What do I want to achieve?"

"Who do I want to spend the rest of my life with?"

"Am I doing a job that I really enjoy?"

"What will I do with my time?"

"If I make this decision who is it likely to affect?"

"Do I like the life I am leading?"

You can reassess your life many times, taking time out to talk to others, spending time alone to think about what you want to achieve or visualise how you would like life to be. Once you make your decision and head along the road – never look back!

Why, you may ask?

The what if scenario never makes progress. You cannot go back, so always move forward with a positive attitude, looking for new opportunities, becoming stronger and wiser from the road already travelled.

What stops you from moving forward, making a decision, making changes or changing the way you do things? **<u>FEAR!</u>**

Several years ago I was working at our local college as a part-time lecturer. The students were fantastic, as were the staff working there. The main problems were the politics, bureaucracy and the sheer volume of paperwork. Talk about draining and depressing. My boss at the time was spiralling down a vortex of depression and, unknown to me, his tension was being passed onto me in the form of migraines. Why didn't I leave? FEAR! Fear of the unknown and fear of letting other people down.

What is fear?
F future
E events
A appearing
R real

Fear is the future predicted through your inner voice, visualisation, dreams and imagination.

- Do you know what will happen in the future?
- How people will react?
- What will be the effect?
- If you will be successful? Etc.

No! - not unless you are a psychic!

Successful people use this in a positive manner. They only see positive outcomes even if in reality it is not as successful as they would have liked – difficulties are seen as opportunities, a way of proving themselves or a chance to change routes. Worried people only see, hear and feel problems ahead so therefore they stand still - seeing a frightening future in front of them and the past behind but unable to make a move.

You will know these people.

"I hate this job – I'm going to look for another." Thirty years later and they are still there, unhappy, stuck on the same rung, bitter and cynical

"I don't love him/her anymore. We've out-grown each other". Thirty years later they only talk in clipped sentences, barely looking at each other and the children rarely visit. Wonder why?"

"I think I'll do more travelling and see the world". Thirty years later the passport is out of date and gathering dust, backpack sold at the car boot sale, postcards from others ripped up and in the bin.

So what stopped these people from moving forward and realising their dream, making a life for themselves and enjoying the things they like doing?

FEAR! Fear of the unknown, fear of what others may say or think, fear of not coping, fear of actually realising the dream. Sad, isn't it!

- What are you afraid of?

- Why?

- What can/are you going to do about it?

- What is the **best** that can happen?

14. In For A Service

I drive a car and every year, according to my service guide and the law, I have to have my car serviced and made road worthy. If we do this with our cars why are we so careless with our bodies and our minds?

Just like the fuel tank you cannot run a bus efficiently if it is not working properly – faulty brakes, broken gasket, slow puncture, no oil etc. It is the same with our bodies.   How can you expect to be travelling down your road if your body is not in good condition?

When was the last time you really had an objective look at what you do?   What you eat and drink, how fit your body is and how far you realistically think your body can take you?

Complete this service check on your health?

How do you rate yourself	Very good	Good	Fair	Poor	Action
Regular exercise e.g. 20 mins 3 times a week					
Healthy eating e.g. 5 portions of fruit and veg a day					
Drinking 2 litres of water a day					
Consuming less salt, sugar, processed food					
Sleeping 8 hours					
Not smoking					
Drinking no more than your recommended units of alcohol per day					

- How road worthy is your health overall?

- What are you going to do to improve?

15. Lay-Bys

What is a lay-by? It is a place to stop, take a rest, look at the view or to have a picnic.

On the road of life a lay-by means exactly the same: taking 'time out'. It can be anything from a holiday, to just taking some time away from the office, home, family etc.

If you do not 'pull over' when you are tired, exhausted or stressed out on a long journey the result could be devastating - a collision, an accident or even death!

The same can be true in life. If you are always on the go - never stopping, not taking holidays, rushing in from work, cooking tea, doing homework, visiting relatives - the results from not taking time out can be disastrous – arguments, extreme tension, migraines, not sleeping, high blood pressure.

You should recognise the signs – you become agitated, depressed and even aggressive. This is the time to pull over, take stock and deep breaths, relax and get ready to carry on the journey.

It does not have to be a two-week holiday in the sun. Dealing with certain stressful situations can be as easy as 4 minutes of deep breathing, a glass of water, a walk in the fresh air or ten minutes listening to music. It is the day-to-day situations that if unrecognised can cause irreparable damage such as heart disease, stroke, even cancer.

I am a full-time working mother and find that the stress of working combined with the added stress of making meals, organising child-minding, collecting from various activities and the usual washing and ironing can sometimes be intolerable, and often like a major expedition. Everyone has similar situations – working and looking after an ageing relative, being on extra committees, illness and so on. All these life situations can cause stress and depression.

Lay-bys for me can be very simple: a long relaxing bubble bath, a good book, a long walk in the country or even a chat on the phone with a friend, just taking time out to rest and relax. Five minutes is sometimes all it takes for me to re-group chill-out and cope with the next pressure on my time.

- What signs do you recognise within yourself that mean you need to pull over to the lay-by?

- How do you know if you need to go into the lay-by?

- What can you do to re-group and chill out?

- What happens if you don't pull over?

16. Bumpy Or Smooth?

As the saying goes "all work and no play makes Jack (and Jill equally) a dull person". It is very apt as it means that other areas of our lives can be neglected. In others words, no work-life balance.

Smoothing out the bumps is having a balance in our lives – not putting too much time, effort and expense into just one area.

On the following table assess each of these areas of your life. Rate yourself from 1 to 10, with 1 meaning very unsatisfied and 10 representing extremely **satisfied,** with how you **feel** within yourself in each section

Score	Family	Friends	Work	"Me" time	Home	Hobbies	Partner
10							
9							
8							
7							
6							
5							
4							
3							
2							
1							

As I wrote this section I completed my table without realising that my house looked like a bomb had hit it! Shoes, books, videos all over the place, no wonder my mind was in a muddle. That weekend I had a massive clear out. Bin bags went out to the rubbish, boxes off to the charity shop and the car was loaded up and taken to the car boot sale (made £145 – not bad!). What a difference. I had smoothed out my road and not only was my house cleaner but my mind had suddenly become clearer and much more focused.

- What segments of your life are out of balance?

- What are/can you do to balance out your bumpy road?

- What is the affect if your road is not smooth?

17. Cruise Control or Conscious?

There have been several instances when I have been driving on a road I know very well, or when I'm deep in thought, and I arrive at my destination thinking – "how did I get here?" "Which road did I take?" You realise that your mind was miles away, almost as if you were not even present. Sad to say I have been like this in my life as well.

There have been times, I hate to admit when I have been out with friends and while I know I am there in body my mind was definitely elsewhere – usually feeling guilty that I was not at home with the family. The same could be said while at work – spending time feeling awful that my children were at the childminder instead of concentrating on what I was supposed to be doing at that time.

I myself have been extremely guilty of not being there in the moment. When my son was younger, I used to play football with him in the back garden. One evening I was kicking the ball back and forwards to my son, not saying a word to him but instead lost in thoughts about work and trying to solve a problem. Suddenly, he picked up the ball and stomped back into the house. "Where are you going?" I asked. "Why do you care" he grumped. "You don't want to be with me, you're somewhere else". He was right, I had hardly said a word to him. I had not asked about his day, offered no encouragement, I had been there in body but not engaged with him in the present.

Where is this lesson taking me you are probably asking yourself? Are you 'present' or are you simply going through the motions on cruise control? Many of us spend too much time focusing on the past or worrying about the future instead of enjoying the present, this moment, here and now not past and future.

If you are with your friends, listen to them, enjoy their company, and concentrate on what they are doing, saying and feeling. If you are at work focus on what you are doing, tune out distractions and pay attention to what is important. What you put in is what you get out of any situation – be conscious!

- What situations are you aware of when you are there in body but not in mind?

- When are you 'not present'?

- Why were you not?

- What are you going to do differently next time?

18. Advertisements

Most buses have advertisements plastered on the sides and the back. Businesses telling the city what they do, what they are good at and why we, the prospective customer, should use them.

Most of us are reserved at telling others what we are good at. Confidence comes from knowing what you do well and focusing on your strengths.

Sometimes we put ourselves down. We either overlook what we are good at or only focus on our weaker qualities. For years I berated myself on the fact that I am useless at paperwork, unable to spell, very disorganised, in fact all the comments that were made to me by my teachers. I feared applying for jobs that I knew I could quite easily do due to my lack of confidence and low self-esteem.

It has taken me years to rid my thoughts of these derogatory remarks, learn to appreciate my abilities and my achievements and realise that education is not just about qualifications. There are other qualities that make us achievers.

It was not until I started to advertise myself that I realised "hey, I am good at some things and in fact not just good – I am very good".

Pretend that you are going to advertise yourself on the side of a bus. Tell others what you are brilliant at.

Start with 10

Good golfer   Great dancer   Very good trainer

Help bring out the best in people   Loyal friend

Creative   Inspiring others   Patient

Good mum/sister/daughter   Being positive

I've done mine, now you do yours!

Ask some of your friends why you are on their bus?   Why do they phone you, ask you out etc? You may find you'll be surprised with the answers.

What did your friends and family say?

Go on add more to your list and keep adding. You never stop going from strength to strength!

19. Hills and Valleys

Hills and valleys are our attitudes – the way we view life and its challenges. Whether we are at the top of the hill – positive, enthusiastic and smiling, or at the bottom of the valley – negative, destructive and critical.

Where you are depends entirely on your attitude!

On a recent walk I stood looking from the valley floor to the top of a very steep Munro (a Scottish mountain over 3000 feet above sea level). A feeling of gloom and, dare I say, hopelessness washed over me. The challenge I had in front of me looked well beyond my reach and in my opinion far too difficult. By the time I had reached the base of the mountain my inner voice had decided that I was definitely NOT going to even attempt this climb. "I'll never do it", "It's far too difficult for me to attempt", "I'm certainly not fit enough" and so on. Did I manage to climb to the top? No! This negative voice had convinced me I'd never accomplish it so why bother trying.

How often do we listen to the voices in our heads and convince ourselves that things are worse than they really are? That we're not good enough, not clever enough etc.

It is amazing how this voice inside our heads can alter our attitude and behaviour.

We can talk ourselves out of just about anything – a putt on the golf course, a tennis match, a job even before you cross the door for the interview.

Negativity is the most destructive behaviour you can possibly have not only for yourself but for others around you.

Standing at the foot of the Munro I had not only convinced myself I would not be able to climb it but I had also passed my negative responses onto my fellow walkers. "If I can't manage it neither will you", "what's the use trying, you're not fit either"

By reacting this way I had managed to pull them into the valley with me and by doing so, had sucked all the energy out of them.

Was I a popular person that day? Whose bus was I on? Not many I can tell you!

However, there were two people in my party that did not let me and my negative attitude pull them down. As Julie said later "I didn't listen to you. I knew inside me that I could do it, I kept saying to myself that you can manage this, you're fit, healthy and hey what a challenge. Think how you'll feel when you make it to the top".

Did they make it? Of course they did and so would I if I had changed my thinking.

That is the difference between hills and valleys - your attitude!

Every day brings us challenges and difficulties and even the smallest non life-threatening situations can have us diving for the tissues, stamping our feet and, more seriously, being destructive and even aggressive towards others e.g.

- Running out of milk
- A person at work off sick
- A car cutting in in front of you
- Rain
- The bus is full
- Asked to send a letter two minutes before leaving for the day

How we react to these situations depends on our internal voices

For example:

The real bus is full.
"Oh well, I'll have to walk – good exercise before work, might meet someone on the way and at least I'm keeping fit".

Or

"Oh, not again! Typical.   Why can't they put on more buses, always happens to me, I'm going to be late again".

The same situation, but different attitude, produces a different reaction to our internal thoughts.

A negative person will focus on things that they cannot change and have no influence or control over. Do they keep their thoughts to themselves? Not usually!

Negative people (drains) throw bombs of destruction wherever they go.

- "That won't work."
- "You can't spell."
- "Don't bother trying, you won't succeed."
- "What are you doing that for? It's a waste of time."

Positive people (radiators), on the other hand, see problems as opportunities, the best in every one and are full of enthusiasm.

- "Yes, I can help you."
- "Fantastic, I knew you could do it."
- "Go on, you can do it."
- "Certainly, I will manage to get that for you."

How can you stay at the top of the hill? Be a radiator?

- Tune into your inner voice.

- Alter your way of thinking.
- Be aware of when you are sinking down the valley. Where do you spend most of your time? At the top or bottom of the valley? **You choose!**
- Focus on the things you can change and not those you can't.

20. Planning Your Route

Why did I start writing this book? While I was waiting one day for Mrs Mitchell, my adopted grandmother, in her Nursing Home, I sat looking around me at all the residents. I thought to myself, how many of them could admit that they had succeeded in achieving what they had set out to do? Or had they even planned to achieve anything at all. I realised at that point that the only thing I had planned for the future was a forthcoming holiday. I had no pension, no idea of where my career was going and no thoughts on the future for my family.

The minute I started to think of the future I started to panic. Would we have enough money? Would my children get into drugs? What if my marriage ended? FEAR was stopping me plan, from looking ahead to the future.

So much so that I would tend to live in the past rather than in the present or plan for the future.

Sitting there in the lounge of the nursing home I realised that I did not want to be there in 40 years time wondering if my life could have been better. I was going to ensure it would be the best I could make it – for all of us!

By planning for the future, mapping my route for success, I could then sit back and enjoy the journey knowing that I had taken control.

I am not so naive as to believe that I can plan the perfect future and see the road ahead. What I can do is have a picture of how I would like to see my life and plan how I can achieve my Vision. This is better than seeing the road ahead as one long empty highway and being scared of what is round the next bend.

- How do you see your future?

- What do you hear people saying to you?

- How will you feel when you have achieved your goals?

- How are you going to make it happen?

- What steps are you going to start today to make it happen?

21. Why are you on the road?

I believe that we are all here on earth for a reason. I was recently asked what my "vision" was for my business.

"To make a positive difference to individuals and organisations" was my reply.

To be perfectly honest until then I hadn't verbalised what my company's vision was. All I knew was that I enjoyed my work which got me up in the morning, gave me my energy and a purpose to my day.

It is not a case of what we do but why we do it.

As I said recently to a security guard at Aberdeen Airport, "Why do you do your job?". "To earn money and pay my mortgage", was his reply.

"No, really" I asked again. "Why do you do what you do?" After thinking long and hard his reply changed. "To ensure my passengers are as safe as possible – and to provide food, shelter and warmth for my family! Wow, I've an important job don't I?"

He had forgotten his purpose in life – have you?

22. Action Plan

As you have read through this book perhaps you have been writing your thoughts or thinking about what actions you intend to do as you proceed down your journey of life.

By writing your thoughts on an action plan this will help prepare you to achieve your aims.

"Remember - we all **think** we can but it's the **doing** that makes the difference"
"Lots of littles make a big….difference"

Action Plan

What is my aim	How will I achieve it?	By when
e.g. To loose 10 Ibs	Enrol at weight watchers Keep a diary of what I eat Walk briskly for half an hour 3 times a week Join the exercise class twice a week	3 months

Signature ....

Date ....

22. Summary

As far as I know we will only be travelling down one road on this earth. Is your bus nearly empty, travelling along a very bumpy road, stopping at very few lay-bys?

Or

Is your bus a full and very happy one, filled with a variety of people smiling and having fun? Is it well fuelled and serviced travelling purposefully forward towards your destination with you in the driving seat?

Which bus is yours?   **You choose!**

Feedback

I would appreciate any comments and feedback.
Please contact me at: anne@stopthebus.org.uk

Acknowledgements

To my mother - without her this guide would have remained on the shelf as an idea not a reality. Thank you for your support, encouragement and belief in me.

To my family and my friends - Jackie Fleming, Lorna Murdoch, Debbie Dickenson, Rebecca Robertson, Michelle Herd, Alf Dunbar and Amanda Fraser. Rhona Dale and Marion Miller who helped edit and correct my English. And so many others who have all listened to me, read my drafts and given me constructive feedback – thank you.

To my family Neil, Katherine and Ross, my brother Alan McKay sister – in - law Debbie

Special thanks to my illustrator Deirdre Varely and proof reader Monique Flecher

www.ingramcontent.com/pod-product-compliance
Lightning Source LLC
Chambersburg PA
CBHW031245280526
45784CB00004B/1719